More Preschool Patterns

EARLY LEARNING TIMESAVERS

by Marilynn G. Barr

Publisher: Roberta Suid
Copy Editor: Annalisa Suid
Design and Production: Marilynn G. Barr
Educational Consultant: Sarah Felstiner

Monday Morning Books is a trademark of
Monday Morning Books, Inc.

ISBN 1-878279-61-0

Printed in the United States of America

9 8 7 6 5 4 3 2

Contents

Contents

Introduction

Welcome to a brand new collection of preschool patterns!

These early learning clips are useful in many ways. They save you, the teacher, that one very precious resource . . . TIME. And this book does more than give you pages and pages of adorable pictures. We've provided you with many ideas about how to use the clips through copying, duplicating, enlarging, etc. to fit your own individual program.

Being a teacher should be fun. But sometimes a busy schedule can overwhelm the joy of educating. That's why you'll find "Teacher Pages" to guide you through a multitude of uses for the following clips.

Start the new school year off on the right foot with cute cubby labels, delightful desk labels, and a collection of seaside name tags that would make Neptune proud. The terrific team tags will help you and your children keep track of small groups. The team suitcase folders make perfect portfolios for you to use when collecting sample art from students, or for students to use to take work home.

Brighten the classroom with activity center labels and spice up bulletin boards, signs, or letters home with pet patterns and the wide variety of useful classroom patterns. The block alphabet patterns make learning fun for students and easy for you, while the holiday patterns focus on interesting events that may sometimes go by uncelebrated: Earth Day, May Day, Chinese New Year, and more.

There are so many ways to work with these creative materials. Read on for a sampling, but don't feel limited by our suggestions. You'll discover dozens of ways to use these clips in your classroom!

TEACHER PAGES

Cubby and desk labels are wonderful ways to help children recognize their space at the start of the year. Some teachers like to enlarge the labels, take Polaroids of the students, and then glue the pictures onto the labels for additional help in cubby recognition. Desk labels can be used the same way. You may want to provide children with matching desk and cubby labels patterns (dragonfly cubby label with dragonfly desk label, for example). Children will enjoy decorating their labels with crayons, chalk, watercolors, or non-toxic markers. The labels also work well for book plates, gift cards, and folder organizers.

Name tags are important for identification during field trips, parent-child open houses, or classroom performances. In some schools, name tags are worn every day by students and teachers alike, and they are always helpful for guest speakers, classroom observers, or volunteers. Laminating, or encasing in Contact paper, will give name tags extra staying power. Allow children the opportunity to decorate their name tags with buttons, cotton balls, beads, sequins, and other craft materials.

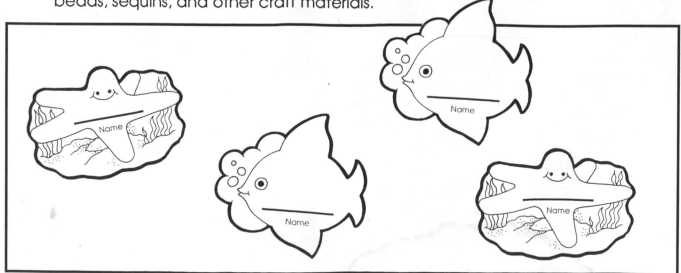

TEACHER PAGES

Team tags are helpful to teachers, visitors, and especially children for identifying small groups. If portfolios of students' work are kept throughout the year (to show parents at conference time), Team Suitcase Folders can be used. Children decorate the patterns which are then attached to manilla folders (or folders made from two pieces of construction paper stapled together). Team Folders can also be used to keep long-term projects together or to bind classroom books (as covers).

Lacing cards give children a chance to practice tying shoes, a ribbon on a present, a roller skate, and a jacket. Have students decorate the patterns with non-toxic markers or crayons, laminate, cover with Contact paper, or Xerox onto card stock, and punch holes in the appropriate places for lasting practice materials.

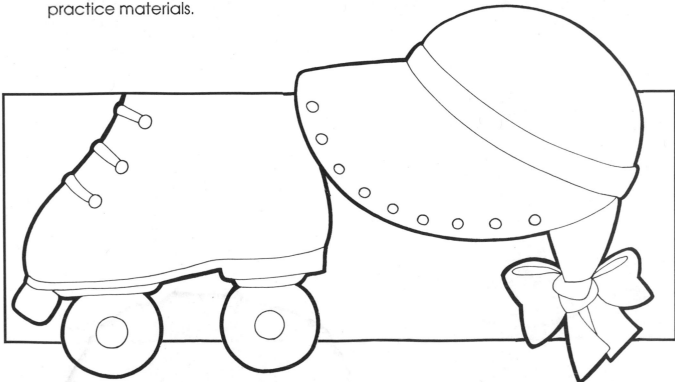

More Preschool Patterns

TEACHER PAGES

Activity center labels help students identify the different curriculum centers in your classroom. The patterns can be decorated by students and then hung by each designated location. If use of an area should be limited to a certain amount of children at a time, you may want to mark this information on the pattern.

The clips collection in <u>More Preschool Patterns</u> includes a variety of bold animal outlines. These patterns can be glued to the front of work folders, or onto construction paper to make cards. Children can decorate the outlines to resemble their own pets, classroom pets, or an animal that they might like to own someday. Provide students with construction paper, colored tissue, fabric scraps, wiggly eyes, sequins, and other decorative materials. Post finished pictures in a classroom pet shop dramatic play corner, or bind in a "My Favorite Animal" classroom book.

The variety of clips found in the useful classroom patterns can be used on bulletin boards, for coloring, or lead-ins for discussions about nature, space, and more.

TEACHER PAGES

Holiday patterns and holiday headband strips help you prepare your students for holidays — both by teaching children about the different important seasonal events, and providing them with ways to work through their new experiences in the classroom. Often holidays aren't REAL for children until AFTER the actual day has gone by. You may find students play-acting Halloween well into November or wanting to give Valentines in June. Exposure to unfamiliar holidays can lead to an open-minded, multiculturally-oriented classroom.

Holiday clips are separated by season, and are perfect for decorating bulletin boards, child-made cards, classroom newsletters, worksheets, and calendars.

Children can color the holiday headband strips, then wear them during holiday celebrations, to greet a new season, or in a classroom parade. Strips can also be linked in chains to decorate the classroom or used to frame paper crafts.

The block alphabet patterns can be colored and posted around the classroom. Give each child a full set of the letters to make individual ABC books, or make it a team effort and create a classroom alphabet book to donate to the school library. The patterns are great for letter recognition, or for beginning tracing practice.

TEACHER PAGES

Fairy tale patterns can be transferred to felt for use during story hour. Or color and cut out the patterns, then glue a small square of felt to the back of each. The patterns may also be made into stick puppet characters. Children will enjoy manipulating their own puppets during the reading of the provided retold stories. These tales have been updated and adapted for the young child, and violent or scary endings and images have been replaced by positive morals. Provide students with the opportunity to make up their own fairy tales using the different figures. Have students decorate the patterns, then glue to Popsicle sticks or drinking straws. A standing theater can be made from a cardboard box. Read children different versions of the fairy tales, and allow them to choose their favorite telling. Additional props may be added from other clips pages.

The Story of Cinderella

A Retold Tale by Annalisa Suid

Once upon a time there lived three sisters. The older two never did anything for themselves. Instead, they made their youngest sister, named Cinderella, do all the chores.

One day, the sisters were invited to a dance at the palace. The older girls made Cinderella iron their dresses and fix their hair.

"You have to do everything," they told her. "We just never learned how." Boy, were they lazy.

By the time the two older sisters were ready to leave for the dance, Cinderella was very dirty and tired from working all day. She hadn't had any time to clean her own dress or wash her own hair.

"Too bad," said her selfish sisters. "You'll just have to stay home." Cinderella sat down on the front stoop and thought about crying. But she was too tired even to cry, and she fell asleep instead. A beautiful fairy appeared to her. The fairy turned Cinderella's messy dress into a sparkling silver gown. She changed a pumpkin into a carriage made of crystal and four little field mice into white, prancing horses.

"What a nice dream," Cinderella said when she woke up. She looked around. There stood the carriage and horses. She was dressed in a lovely gown and her hair was piled high on her head and decorated with diamonds.

"Go to the ball," the fairy told Cinderella, for the fairy was real, too. "But be sure to be home by midnight. Do you know how to tell time?"

"Yes." Cinderella said. Even though her sisters had never bothered to learn, Cinderella knew that twelve o'clock was when both the little hand and the big hand pointed to twelve.

Cinderella had a wonderful time at the ball. She even danced with the prince, but at ten minutes to midnight she told him that she had to go home. He was so impressed that she knew how to tell time, that he took her home himself. The fairy was waiting for them by Cinderella's door.

"I'm glad you made it home in time," the fairy told her, "And because you're such a hard worker, I think you should live happily ever after." So Cinderella and the prince got married. They both took care of the castle together. Cinderella taught the prince how to do laundry and mow the lawn. Since they shared the chores, they had lots of free time to have fun. But Cinderella's selfish sisters were helpless. Their house grew so dirty that none of their friends would come by.

Cinderella felt sad that her sisters were so unhappy. So she and the prince came over to teach her sisters how to take care of themselves.

Fairy Tale Patterns
Cinderella Characters & Props

More Preschool Patterns

Fairy Tale Patterns
Cinderella Characters & Props

Fairy Tale Patterns
Cinderella Characters & Props

More Preschool Patterns

The Story of Hansel and Gretel

A Retold Tale by Annalisa Suid

Once upon a time there lived a brother named Hansel and a sister named Gretel who both loved junk food. They never ate the good lunches that their father prepared for them. They would trade their peanut butter sandwiches for cupcakes and candy.

One day, on their way home from school, the children decided to take a shortcut and they got lost. They wandered further and further away from their home until they were in a dark forest.

"I think this is an enchanted forest," said Gretel.

"Why do you think so?" asked Hansel.

"Well, just look over there." Gretel pointed to a house that stood in a small clearing. The house was made entirely of gingerbread, with spun sugar windows, a licorice chimney, and lollipops lining the front path.

"Great!" said Hansel, "I'm hungry!"

"Me, too," said Gretel, and they started to eat the cookie roof.

Suddenly, a lady came out of the house. She pretended to be nice to the children. She gave them each a huge bag of candy, and then tucked them into warm, cozy beds. But she was really very grumpy and unhappy from eating too many sweets. She wanted to make the children sick with candy so that they wouldn't be able to play anymore and they would have to work for her, scrubbing, painting, and weeding the garden.

After the third day of eating nothing but junk food, Gretel told Hansel she didn't feel very well. While they were working in the grumpy lady's garden, Hansel took some vegetables and put them in his pockets. That night, instead of eating candy, he and Gretel ate vegetables. The next day they ate fruit off the trees. Within a week of eating healthy, they felt well enough to run away, and they escaped and made their way home. The grumpy lady watched them run away.

"They certainly do look healthy," she said to herself. "Maybe I ought to start eating some vegetables, too."

The children's parents were very happy to see them. In fact, they were so happy, they took Hansel and Gretel out to an ice cream shop to buy them a triple-decker, chocolate fudge, whipped-cream covered sundae.

"No, thanks," Hansel and Gretel said together. "Could we just have some fruit instead? Healthy food makes us feel better."

Fairy Tale Patterns
Hansel & Gretel Characters & Props

16

Fairy Tale Patterns
Hansel & Gretel Characters & Props

Candy

     More Preschool Patterns

More Preschool Patterns

The Story of Sleeping Beauty

A Retold Tale by Annalisa Suid

Once upon a time there lived a very curious princess who liked to wander around the castle examining objects and learning their uses.

"What's that?" she asked the cook who was cutting vegetables.

"This is a very sharp knife," the cook told her. "You must be careful when cutting with something this sharp."

The princess wandered into her older sister's room. Her sister was cutting hearts out of construction paper for Valentines.

"What are those?" the little princess asked.

"These are scissors," her sister said. "They're very sharp; you must only use your small scissors when you want to cut something."

The princess spent all of her free time learning about everything in the castle. She became very smart. One day, when she was sixteen, she decided to climb the stairs that led to the tallest tower in the kingdom. At the very top room she found a weaver spinning thread.

"What's that?" she asked the weaver.

"This is a spindle," the weaver told her. "It has a very sharp point. Be careful not to prick yourself."

The princess had never seen a spindle before. She was very curious about it, and bent closer to get a better look. By accident, she pricked her finger. If it had been a normal spindle, the princess would only have needed a band-aid to make her feel better. But this was an enchanted spindle, and when the princess pricked her finger she fell asleep for one hundred years. The spell was so strong, that the entire palace fell asleep.

One day, one hundred years later, a prince happened to be riding by the castle. He heard loud snores coming from behind the walls, and, since he was a curious prince, he stopped his horse so he could take a look. He walked through the rooms of the palace. Finally, he reached the bedroom of the sleeping princess. She looked so lovely that he couldn't resist giving her a kiss. Instantly, she opened her eyes, for the kiss broke the spell.

"Wow," said the princess, "What a strange dream I had."

"About what?" asked the curious prince.

When she finished telling her story, the prince said, "I can't believe that I've found a girl who is as curious about things as I am! I think that we should go explore the world and see what we can find."

"That sounds marvelous," said the princess. They walked hand in hand out of the palace on their way to discovering many wonderful new things.

Fairy Tale Patterns
Sleeping Beauty Characters & Props

20

Fairy Tale Patterns
Sleeping Beauty Characters & Props

Fairy Tale Patterns
Sleeping Beauty Characters & Props

More Preschool Patterns

The Story of the Frog Prince

A Retold Tale by Annalisa Suid

Once upon a time there lived a very beautiful princess who had a golden ball that was her favorite toy. One day, while she was tossing her ball in the air, it rolled into a pond. The princess began to cry. Luckily, a tiny frog hopped out of the water and offered to get her ball for her. In return, the frog wanted to be the princess's best friend.

The princess agreed to be friends with the frog, even though he was an ugly frog, because she really wanted her ball back. The frog hopped into the water and found the ball. Instead of thanking the frog for helping her, the princess ran home to the castle, much faster than the frog could jump.

That night, at dinner, there was a knock on the door. When the princess opened it up, there sat the little frog.

"You promised to be my friend," the frog said.

The princess was very upset to see the frog. She thought the frog was slimy and yucky. Her father, the King, asked her what was wrong, and when she told him the story, he said, "You can't break your promise to the frog."

So the princess took the frog into the castle. She had dinner with it, and then they played a game of checkers. The frog was a very good player. When it was time to go to bed, the frog hopped onto the princess's shoulder, and rode all the way up to her bedroom. He told her funny jokes that made her laugh. Soon she forgot that he was just an ugly old frog.

"Do you want to sleep with a night light on?" she asked the frog.

"No, I'm not scared of the dark since I've found such a good friend."

They said goodnight, and climbed into the princess's bunk beds.

"I'm glad that I've found such a good friend, too," the princess said to the frog. She leaned down from her top bunk and gave him a goodnight kiss. Suddenly, there was a flash of light and the frog changed into a very nice looking prince.

"Wow!" said the princess. "What happened?"

"I was changed into a frog because I never took the time to make friends with people who didn't look the same as I did," the frog told her. "You learned to like me, not for how I look, but for how I am, and that broke the spell."

"That's neat," said the princess. "But I don't care whether you are a prince or a frog. Tomorrow I'm going to beat you at checkers!"

"You can try," said the Frog Prince.

And they were best friends forever.

Fairy Tale Patterns
The Frog Prince Characters & Props

Fairy Tale Patterns
The Frog Prince Characters & Props

More Preschool Patterns

Fairy Tale Patterns
The Frog Prince Characters & Props

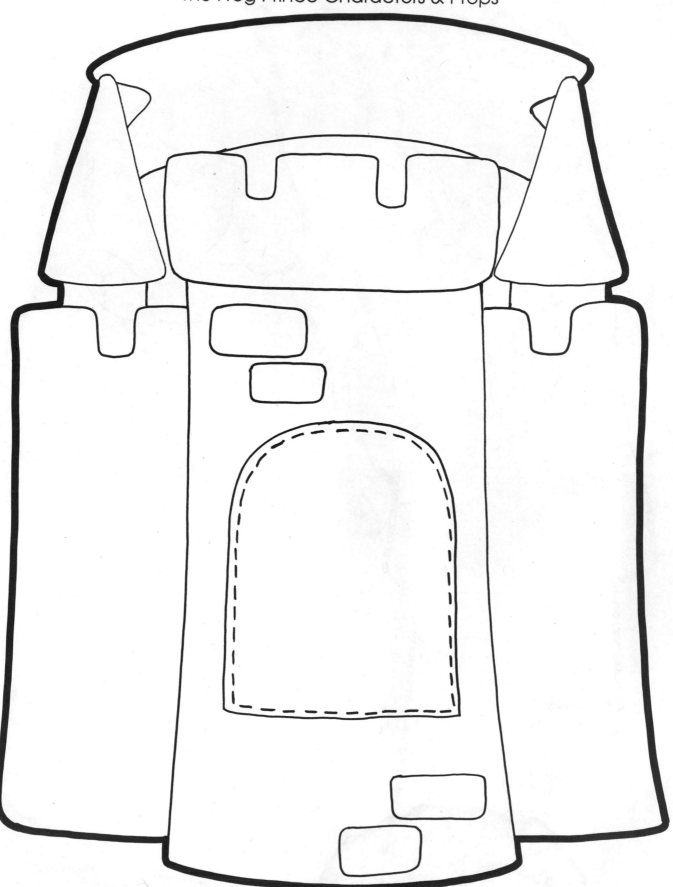

More Preschool Patterns

Cubby Labels
Dragonflies

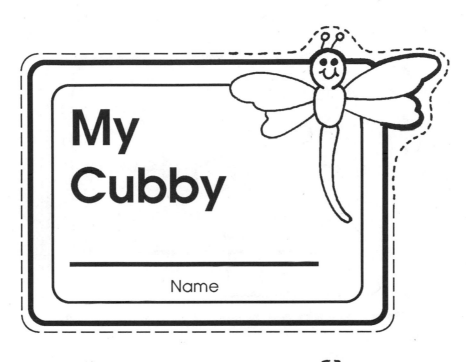

My
Cubby

_____

Name

My
Cubby

_____

Name

Cubby Labels
Ladybugs

My
Cubby

_____

Name

My
Cubby

_____

Name

My
Cubby
_____
Name

My
Cubby
_____
Name

Cubby Labels
Caterpillars

My
Cubby

_____

Name

My
Cubby

_____

Name

My
Cubby

_____
Name

My
Cubby

_____
Name

Desk Labels
Dragonflies

My
Desk

_____

My
Desk

_____

My
Desk

_____

My
Desk

_____

My
Desk

_____

My
Desk

_____

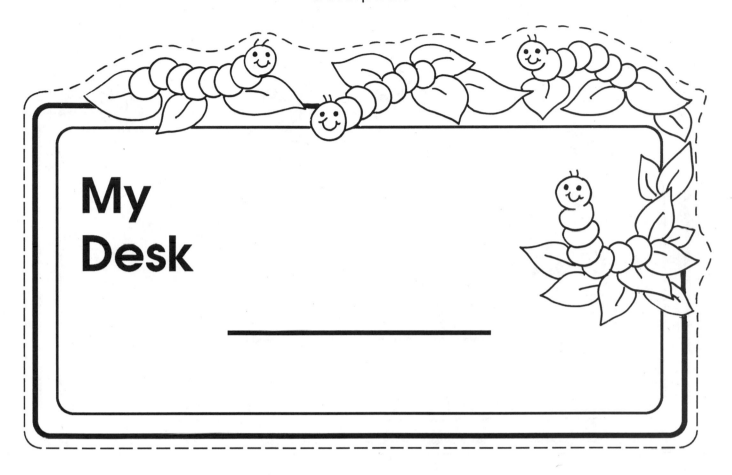

My
Desk

_____

My
Desk

_____

My
Desk

_____

My
Desk

_____

Name Tags
Angelfish

39 More Preschool Patterns

Name Tags
Starfish

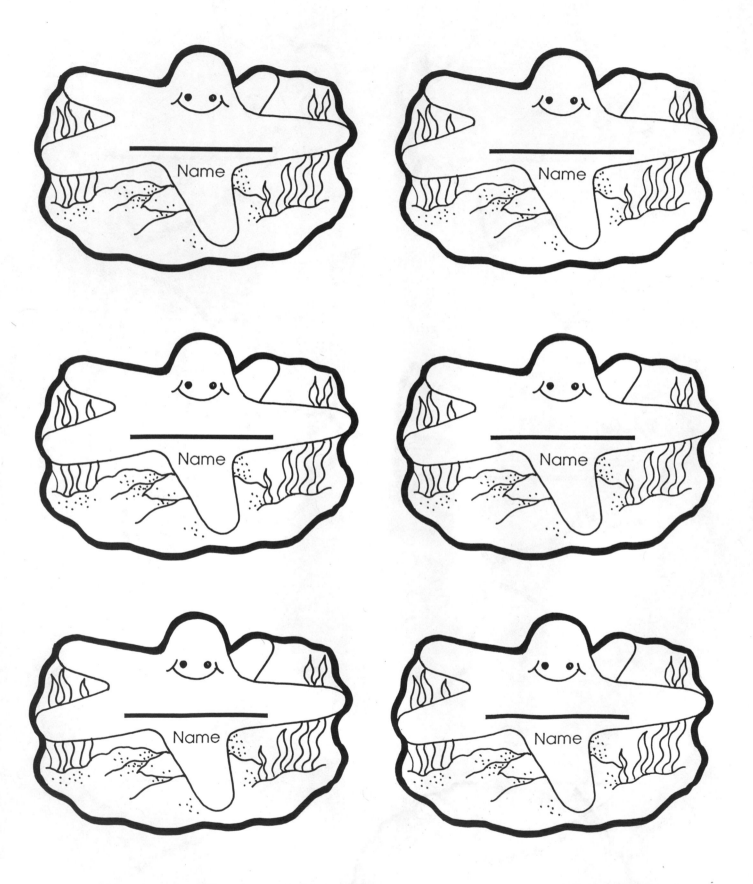

Name Tags
Octopus

Name

Name

Name

Name

Name

Name

More Preschool Patterns

Name Tags
Sea Horses

Name

Name

Name

Name

Name

Name

More Preschool Patterns

Name Tags
Whales

Name

Name

Name

Name

Name

Name

 More Preschool Patterns

Name Tags
Sea Turtles

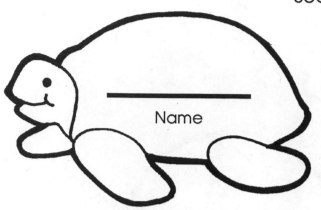

Name

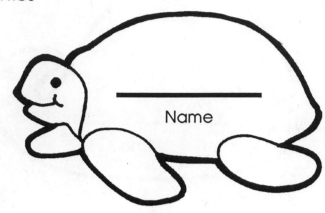

Name

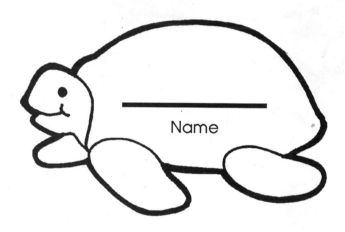

Name

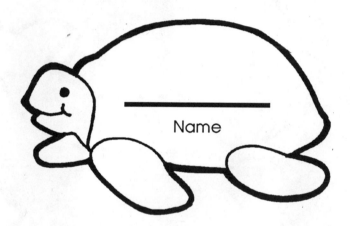

Name

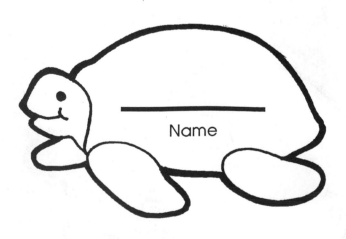

Name

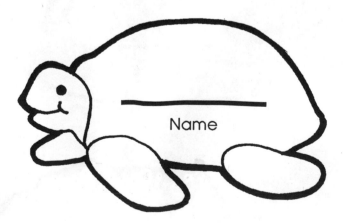

Name

More Preschool Patterns

Name Tags
Seashells

Name

Name

Name

Name

Name

Name

More Preschool Patterns

Name Tags
Jellyfish

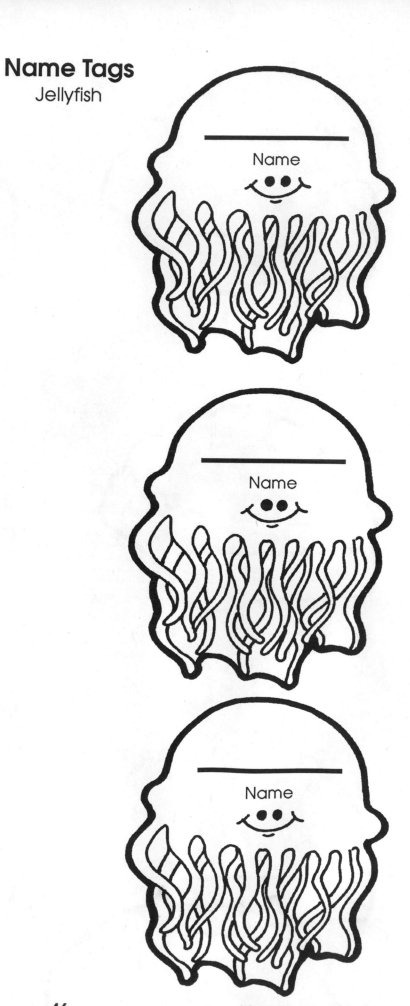

Name

Name

Name

Name

Name

Name

More Preschool Patterns

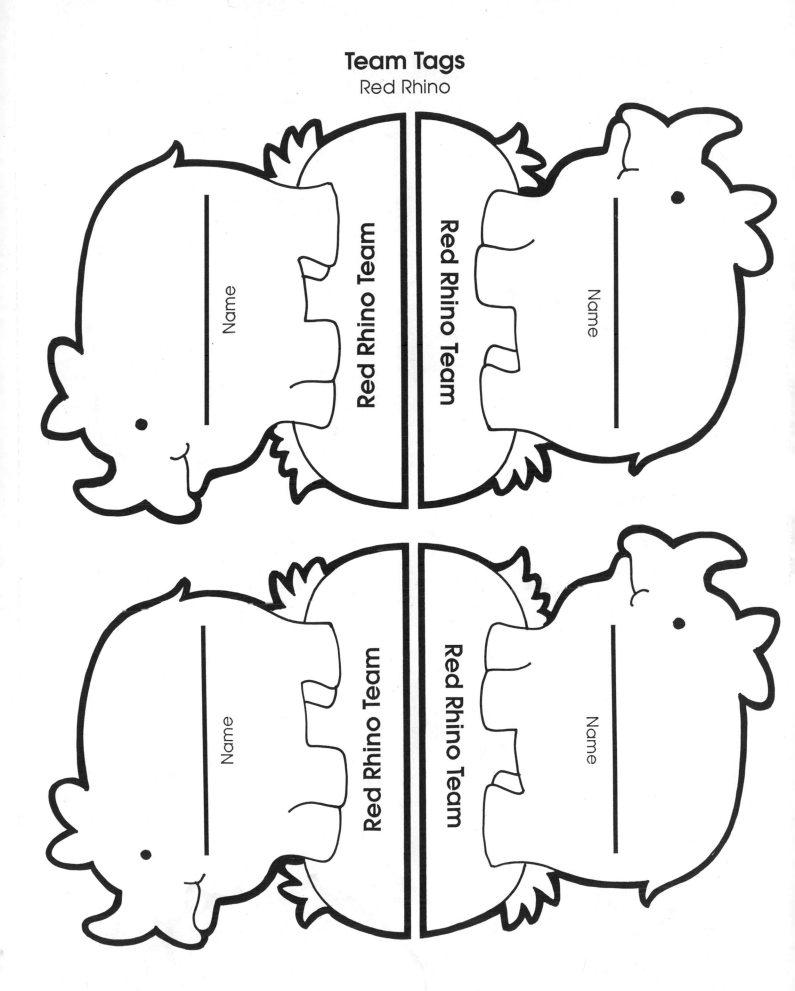

Name

Red Rhino Team

Red Rhino Team

Name

Name

Red Rhino Team

Red Rhino Team

Name

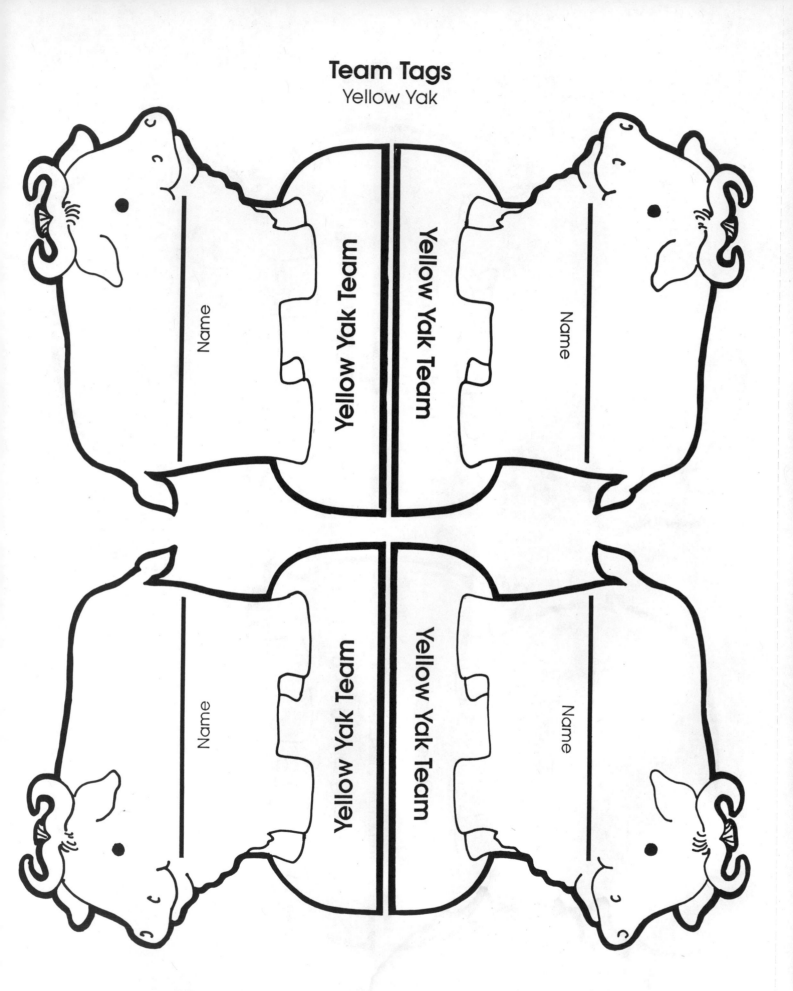

Name

Yellow Yak Team

Yellow Yak Team

Name

Name

Yellow Yak Team

Yellow Yak Team

Name

More Preschool Patterns

Green Gorilla Team

Green Gorilla Team

Name

Name

Green Gorilla Team

Green Gorilla Team

Name

Name

49

More Preschool Patterns

Team Tags
Blue Kangaroo

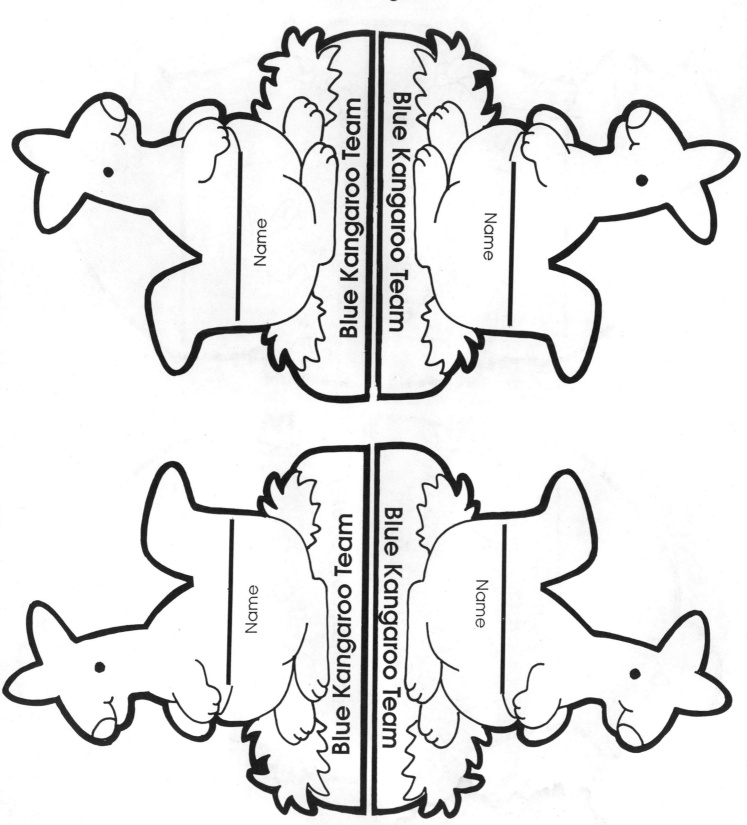

Blue Kangaroo Team

Blue Kangaroo Team

Name

Name

Blue Kangaroo Team

Blue Kangaroo Team

Name

Name

50

More Preschool Patterns

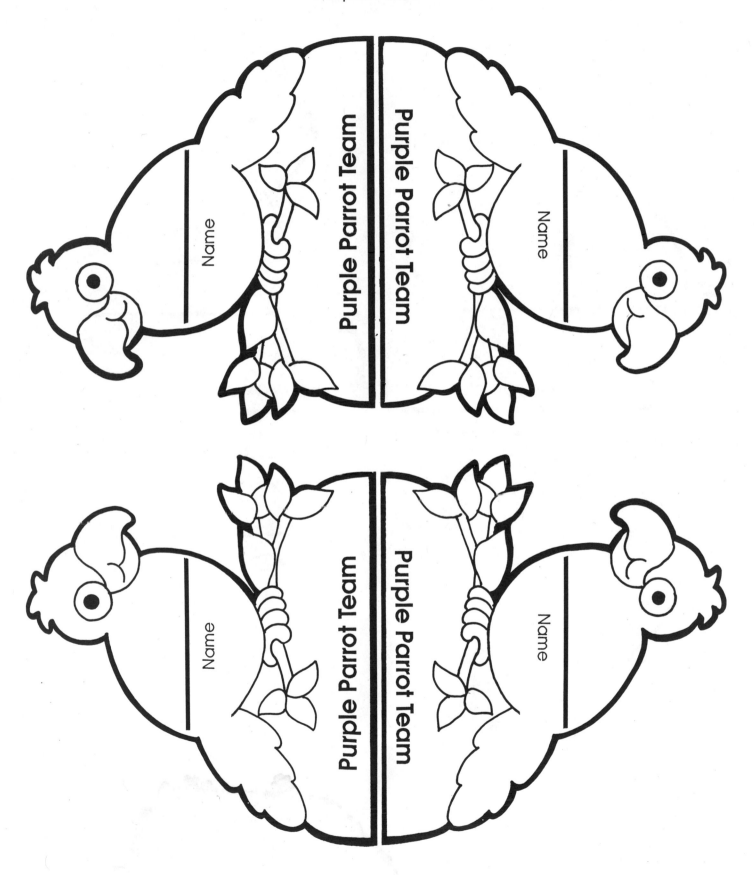

More Preschool Patterns

Team Tags
Brown Bear

Name

Brown Bear Team

Name

Brown Bear Team

Brown Bear Team

Name

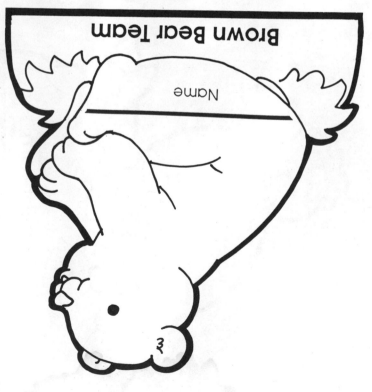

Brown Bear Team

Name

More Preschool Patterns

Team Suitcase Folders
Red Rhino's Suitcase

Team Suitcase Folders
Yellow Yak's Suitcase

More Preschool Patterns

Team Suitcase Folders
Green Gorilla's Suitcase

Team Suitcase Folders
Blue Kangaroo's Suitcase

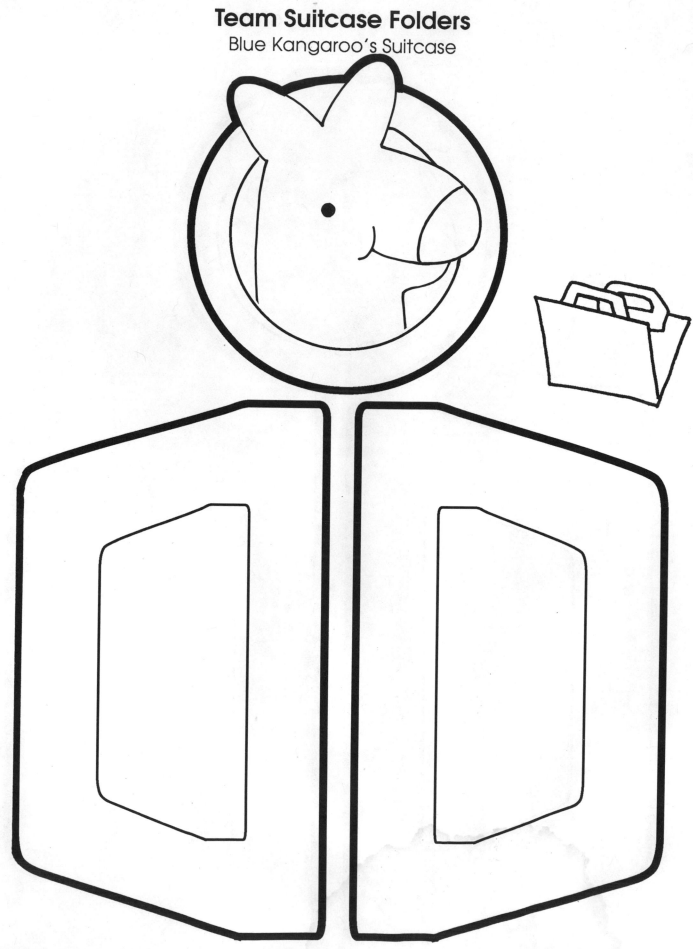

56

More Preschool Patterns

Team Suitcase Folders
Purple Parrot's Suitcase

Team Suitcase Folders
Brown Bear's Suitcase

58

Lacing Cards
Quilt Square

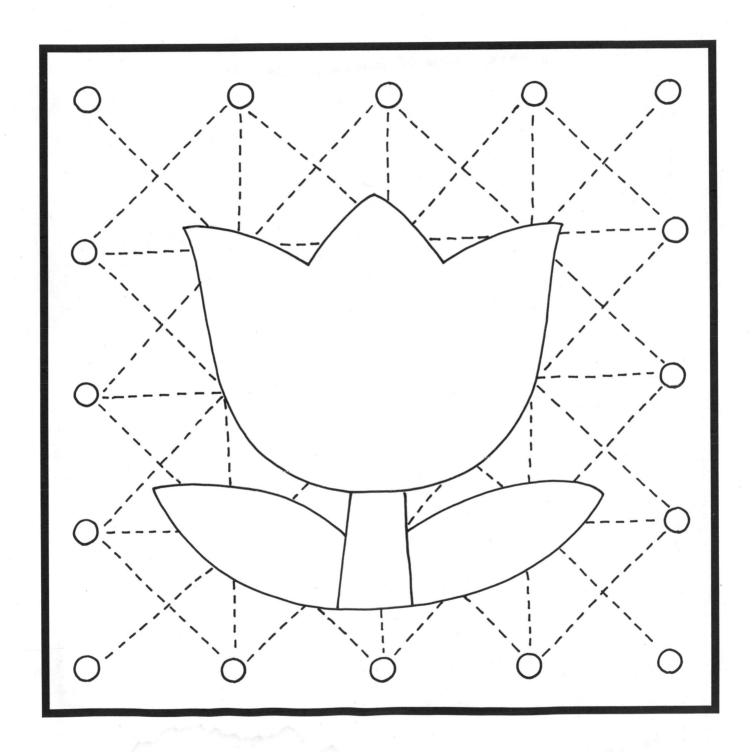

Lacing Cards
High Top Boot

More Preschool Patterns

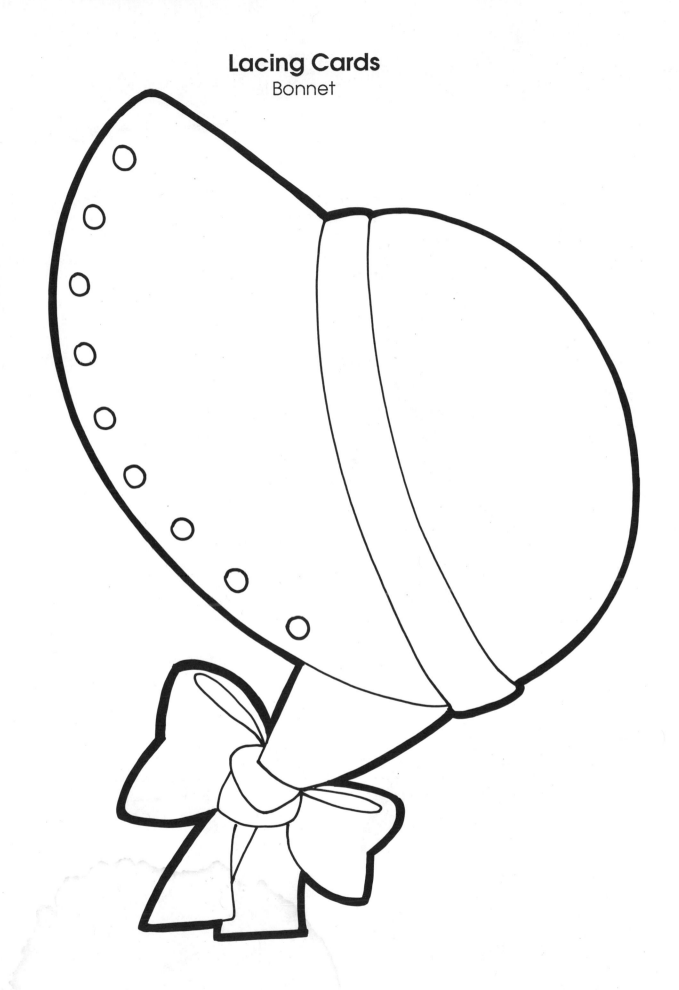

Lacing Cards
Roller Skate

62

More Preschool Patterns

Lacing Cards
Jacket

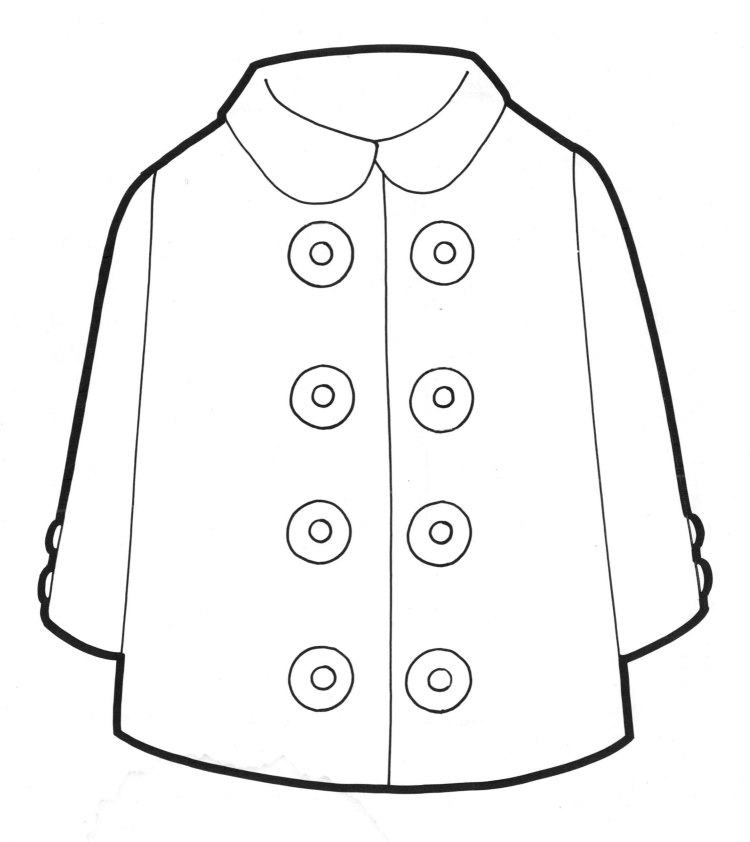

63

More Preschool Patterns

Lacing Cards
Present

More Preschool Patterns

69

Aesop's Fables

Peter Pan

Nursery Songs

ALL ABOUT ABC's

MOTHER GOOSE RHYMES

Grimm's Fairy Tales

The Library

My Pet Kitten

73

More Preschool Patterns

Pet Patterns
Puppy

My Pet Puppy

More Preschool Patterns

My Pet Bird

Pet Patterns
Hamster

My Pet Hamster

Pet Patterns
Goldfish

My Pet Goldfish

GOLD FISH FOOD

My Pet Bunny

My Pet Turtle

TURTLE FOOD

Pet Patterns
Guinea Pig

My Pet Guinea Pig

Useful Classroom Patterns
Birds

More Preschool Patterns

Useful Classroom Patterns
Rocket Ships

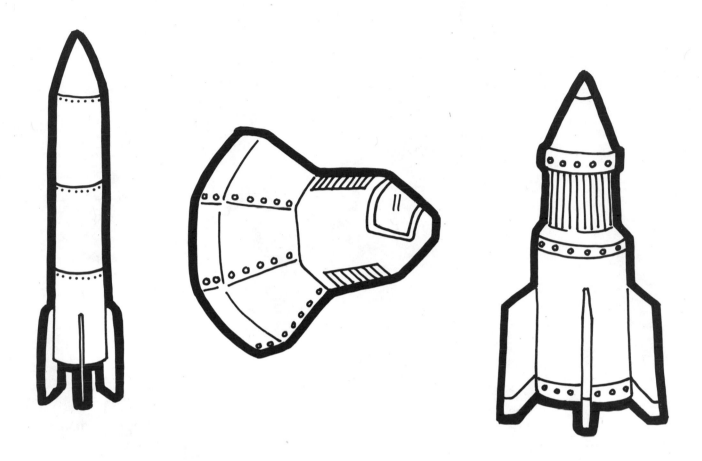

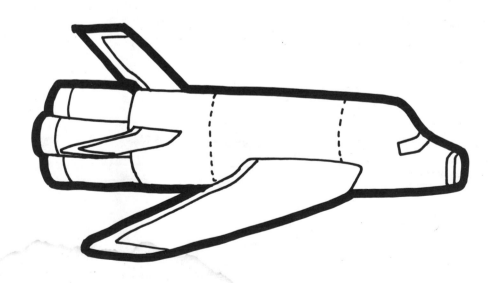

More Preschool Patterns

Useful Classroom Patterns
Planes

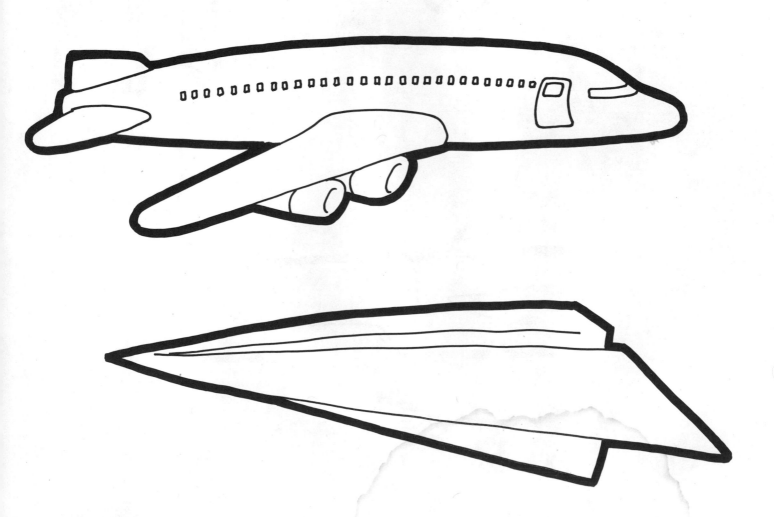

More Preschool Patterns

Useful Classroom Patterns
Stars

More Preschool Patterns

Useful Classroom Patterns
Paper Doll (male)

Useful Classroom Patterns
Mask

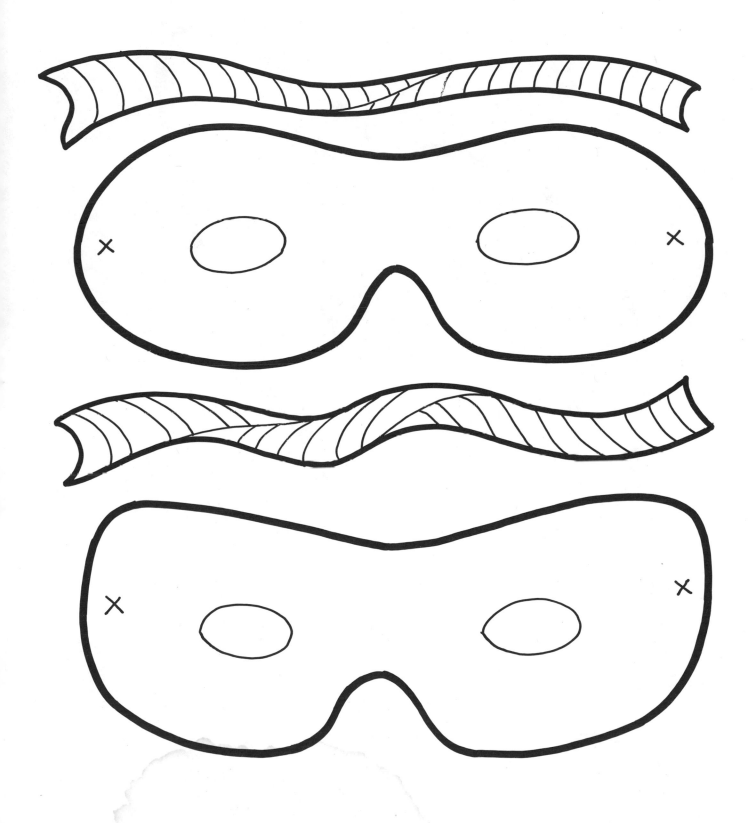

More Preschool Patterns

Useful Classroom Patterns
Saturn

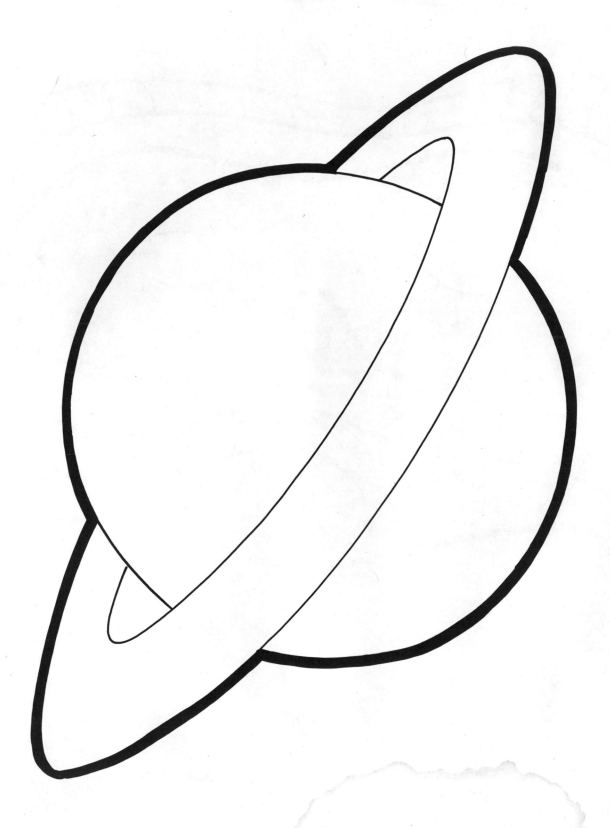

More Preschool Patterns

Autumn

Holiday Patterns
Fall

More Preschool Patterns

More Preschool Patterns

95

More Preschool Patterns

Holiday Headband Strips
Harvest

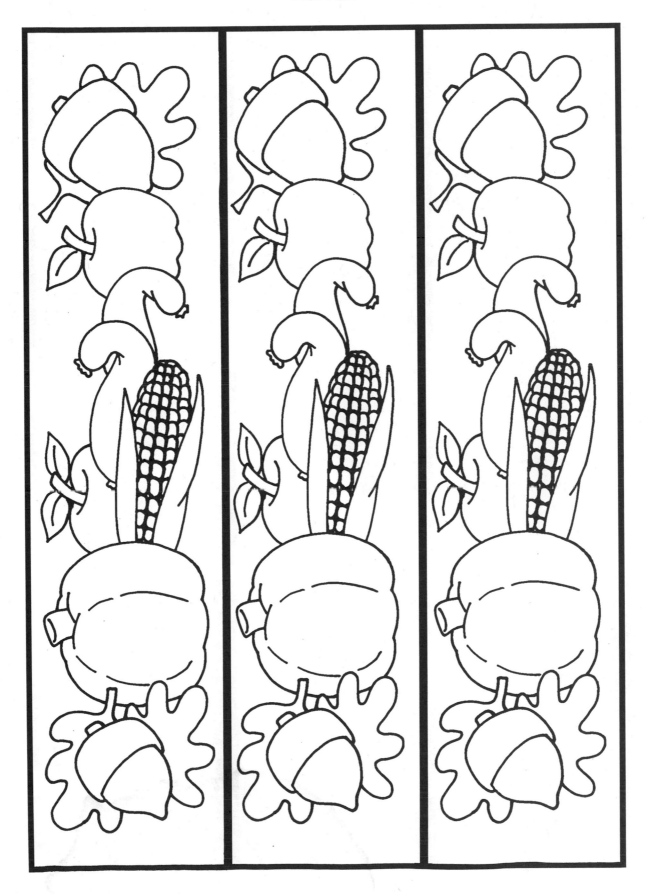

Holiday Headband Strips
Reindeer

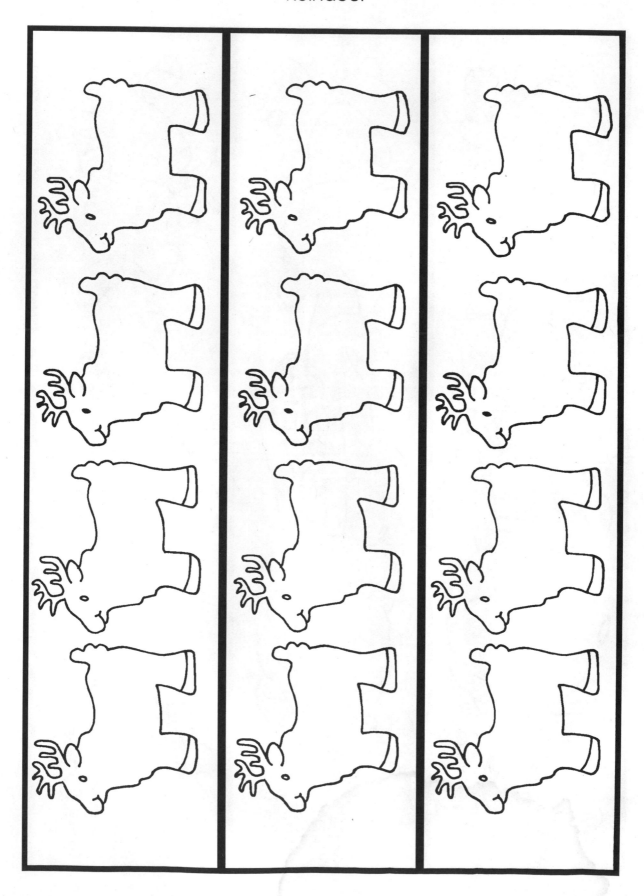

More Preschool Patterns

Holiday Headband Strips
Valentine

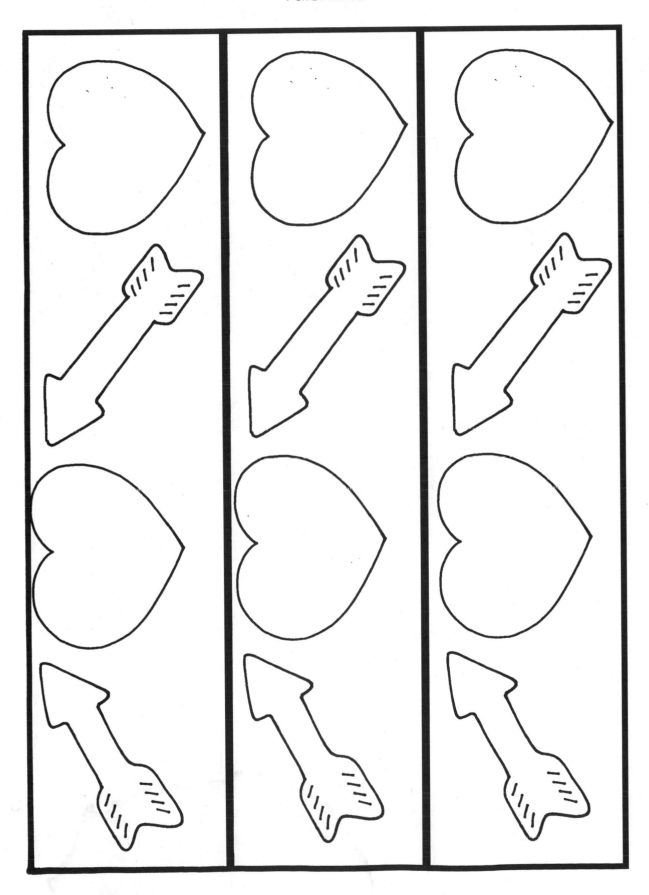

More Preschool Patterns

Holiday Headband Strips
Earth Day

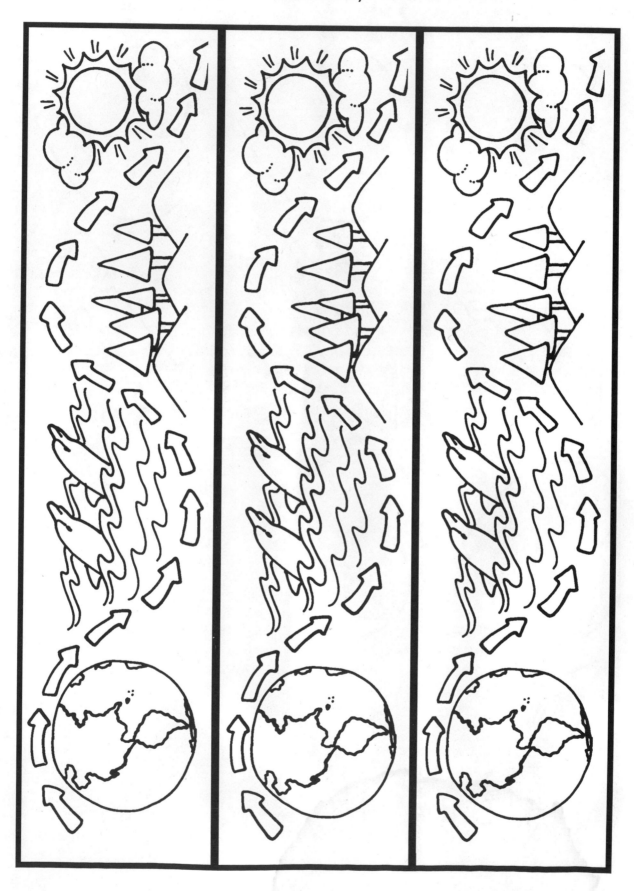

More Preschool Patterns

Holiday Headband Strips
May Day

Holiday Headband Strips
Vacation

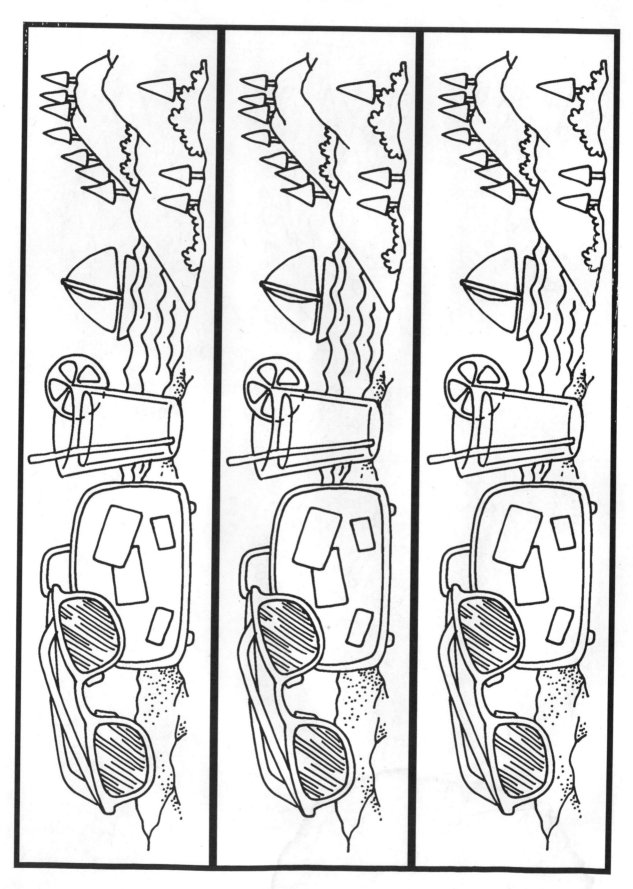

Block Alphabet Patterns

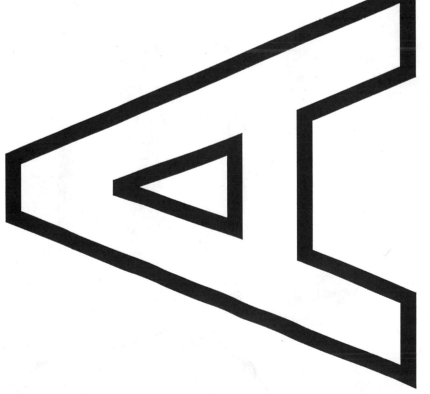

103   More Preschool Patterns

Block Alphabet Patterns

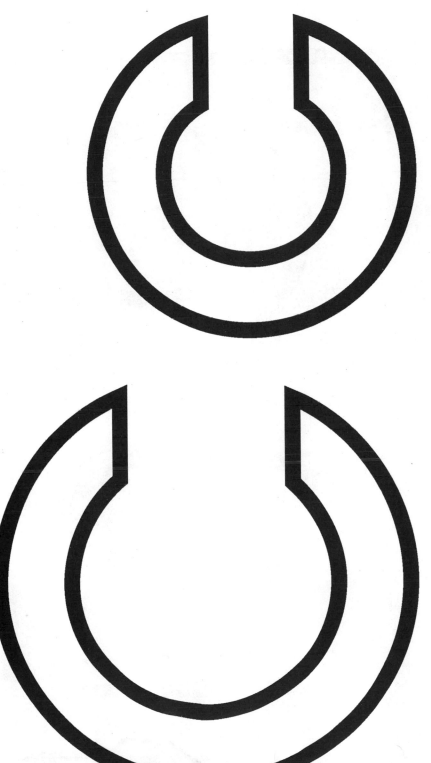

Block Alphabet Patterns

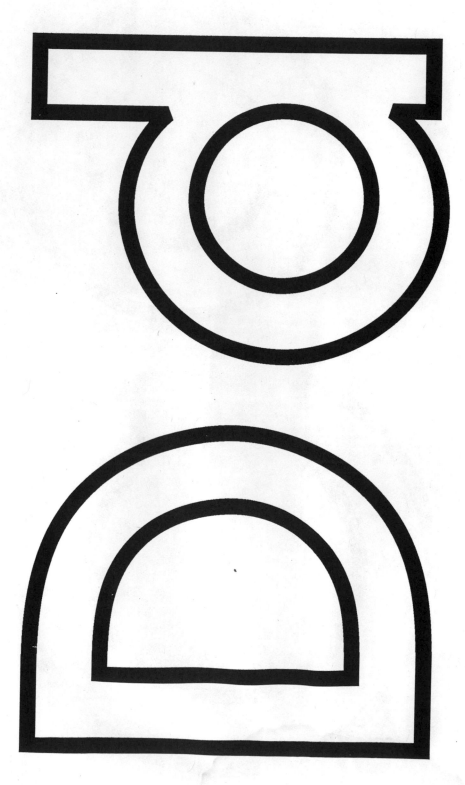

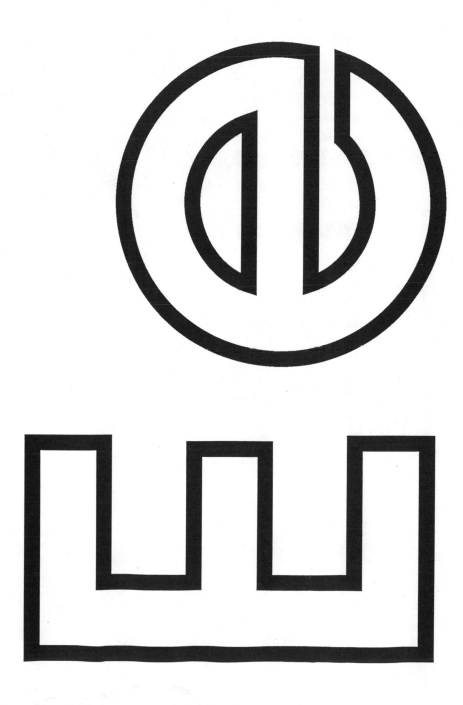

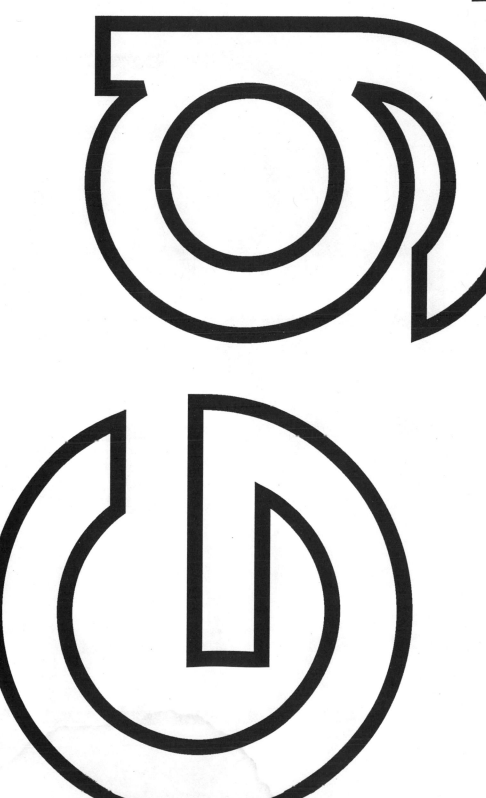

More Preschool Patterns

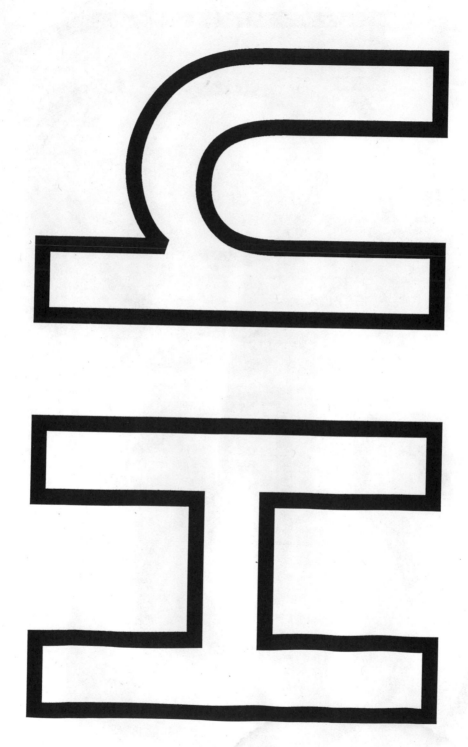

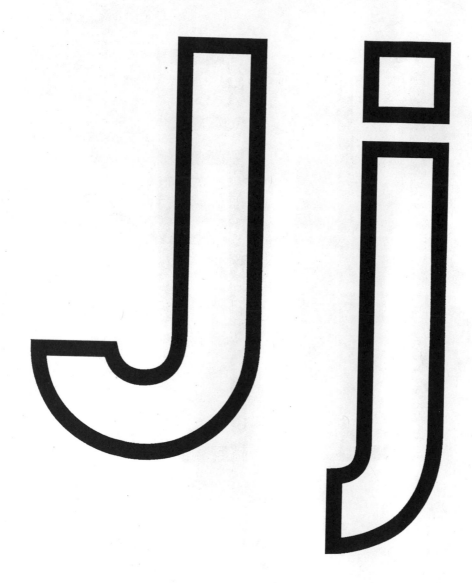

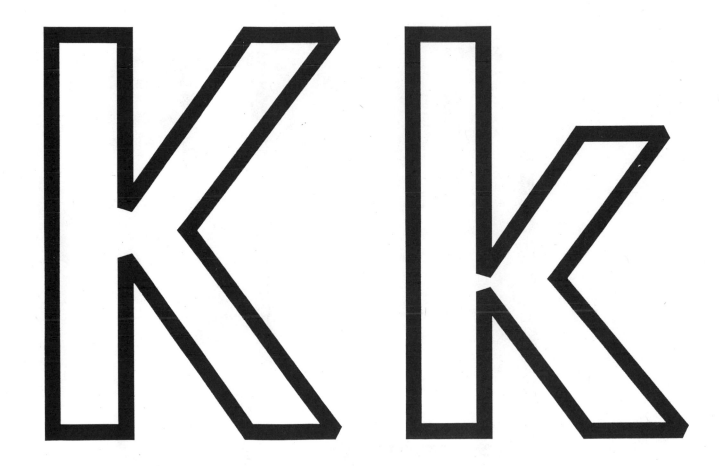

More Preschool Patterns

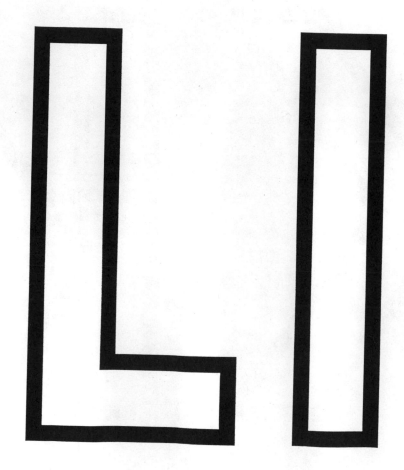

M

Block Alphabet Patterns

Block Alphabet Patterns

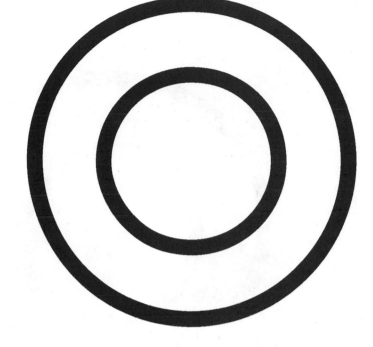

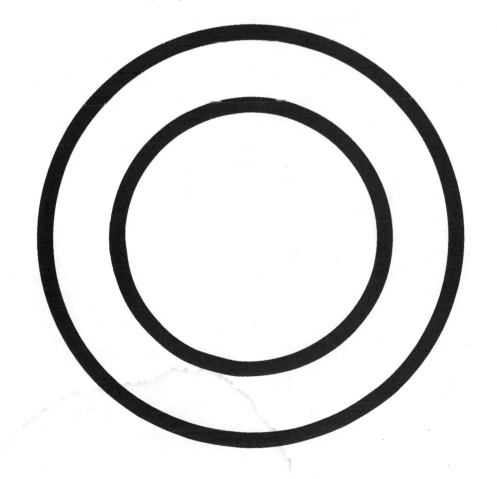

More Preschool Patterns

Block Alphabet Patterns

Block Alphabet Patterns

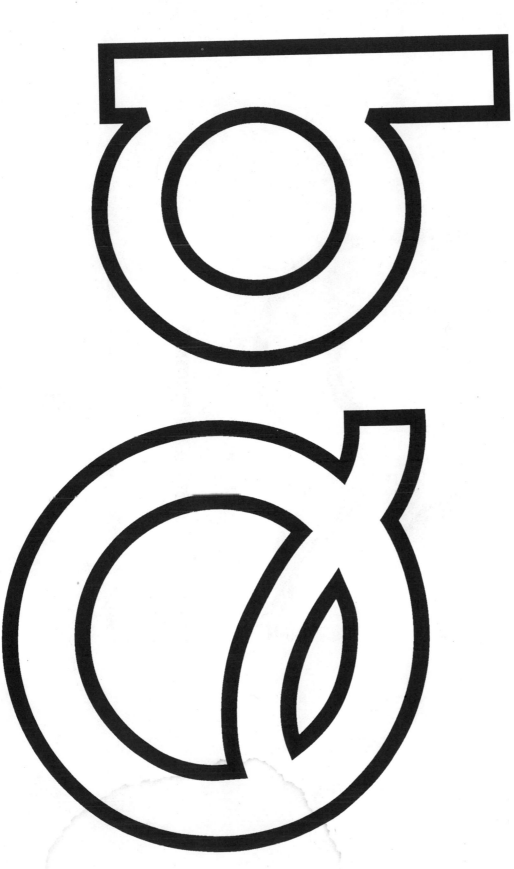

Block Alphabet Patterns

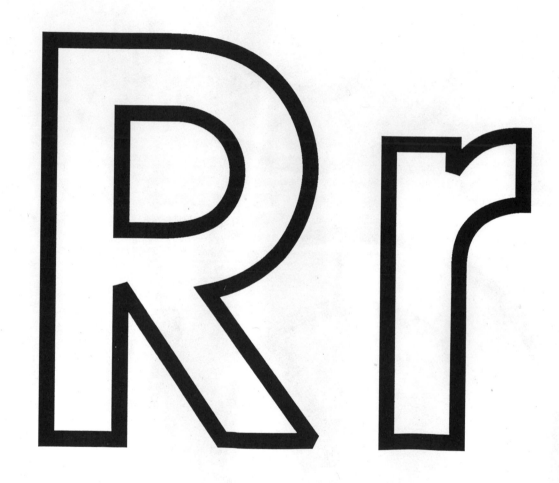

Block Alphabet Patterns

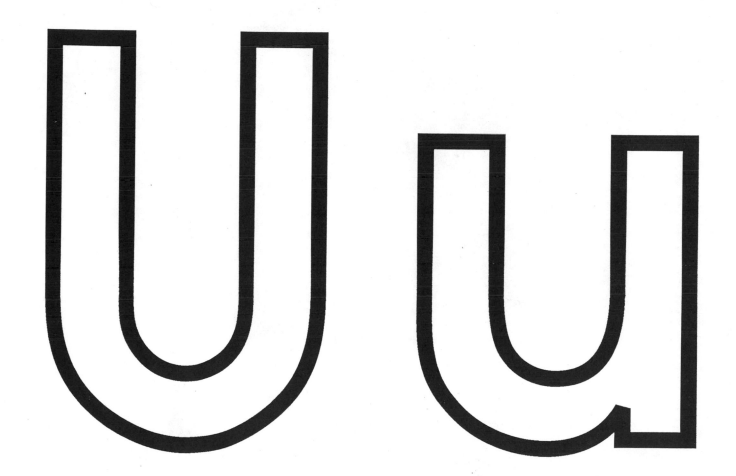

Block Alphabet Patterns

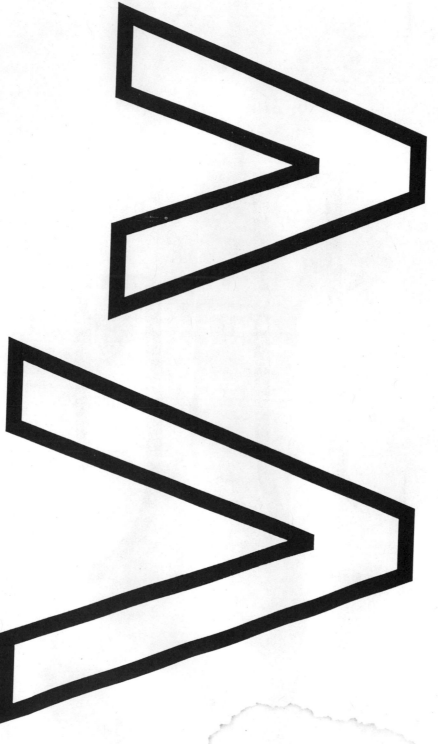

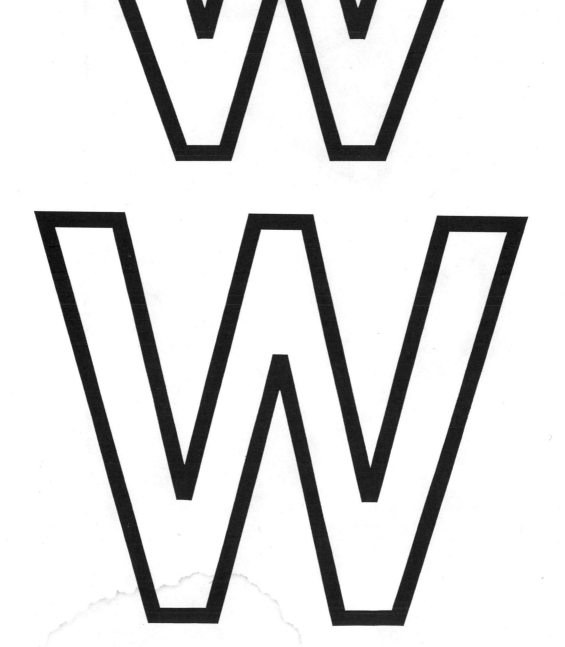

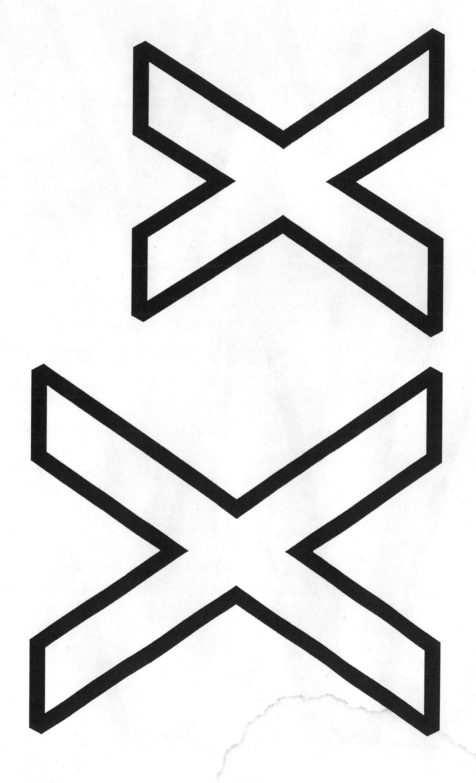

Block Alphabet Patterns

More Preschool Patterns